ROAD LEADING INTO ETERNITY

ROAD LEADING INTO ETERNITY

Seeking Intimacy with God

John 14:6 NEV "Jesus answered,
'I am the way, and the truth, and the life.
The only way to the Father is through me....

By: William B. Hatch

XULON PRESS

Xulon Press
2301 Lucien Way #415
Maitland, FL 32751
407.339.4217
www.xulonpress.com

Paperback ISBN-13: 978-1-6628-3588-9
Ebook ISBN-13: 978-1-6628-3589-6

This book is dedicated to my wonderful wife, Judith E. Hatch, who has been a tremendous influence in how my faith has developed over the past fifty years.

TABLE OF CONTENTS

ACKNOWLEDGMENTS

Jeff Schoess, who has provided the equipment necessary to write the manuscript. He is a supportive friend whose love for the Lord exceeds many. As a disciple of men, he is my example to follow, as I am also a disciple of men.

Pastor Don Reigstad, a true man of God. His vast knowledge of scriptures contributes to his ability to tell biblical stories and makes real application of the stories into daily living. His knowledge of God is totally amazing. Needless to say, he is a great preacher.

Pastor Jim Brown, a living Barnabus. He is a great encourager, helping me to see the real worth that I am to Jesus Christ. He is a man of great love for the people he serves.

James and Debbie Long. They are my reminders that I truly belong to Jesus Christ. They are humble servants for the Lord and are generous in their giving. They are true friends, and a dear brother and sister in Jesus Christ.

Stewart Hatch, for purchasing a new computer, to enable me to communicate better with my publisher.

Donny Turvold, for helping me to understand better how to navigate the computer and the Word program.

TESTAMENT OF CHARACTER

"Bill Hatch is one of the most genuine people I know. His sensitivity to both GOD and people is commendable. The genuineness of soul and the sensitivity of his spirit come through his writing. I commend him and his writing to anyone who seeks a godly authenticity in this world of plastic spirituality." (*Senior Pastor Don Reigstad*, Lincoln Evangelical Free Church.)

"I met Bill Hatch at Lincoln Evangelical Free Church where he has been a faithful member and a willing servant. Bill loves the Lord, his wife, his family, and his church family. As we have spent time together in small groups and other fellowship opportunities, I have been privileged to observe that Bill is a God-fearing man who seeks to live by the teachings and principles of God's Word, the Bible." (*Jim Brown*, Community Life Pastor.)

"I fell in love with Bill when I have read his writings, when we were courting each other." (*Judith E. Hatch*—his wife.)

"In order to love others unconditionally, one must first be loved by Christ. As I silently watch Bill live out his life, tenderly caring for those around him, clinging to the promised unseen for hope, trusting in our risen Savior for daily strength, I am certain he knows he is loved by Christ. He brings encouragement, joy, and strength to me. It is an honor and privilege to know and enjoy fellowship with him." (*Debbie Long*, Homemaker who loves Christ and a good friend.)

"A book on poetry that is thoughtful, inspiring, and a joy to read. Honest, deep, wise. Warmly recommended." (*Jeff Schoess*, President and CEO of Eden Medical, Inc. Howard Lake, Minnesota, and best friend.)

INTRODUCTION:

This is a collection of poems, prayers, and devotionals designed to capture the hearts of all who desire to come closer to God, seeking His love, mercy, and grace.

There are four sections:

Section One: Road Leading Into Eternity—a collection of writings that gives testimony of Jesus Christ and His ministry of bringing salvation to all of mankind.

Section Two: Revelation Song—is a collection of poems and prayers, which reflects the Great Tribulation, the Millennium, and the New Creation.

Section Three: In Living for Christ—is a collection of poems depicting life as a Christian.

Section Four: Discovering God's Wisdom—is four poems that reflects upon God's wisdom in daily living.

Opening Prayer.

O' Lord, and our God, as we come before Your throne, being drawn to You by Your one and only begotten Son, let our eyes be fixed upon Him—Who is our Savior, and Friend. May Your Holy Spirit comfort us as He dwells within us and seals us to be Yours forever as we travel into Eternity. In the name of Your precious Son, Jesus, The Messiah. Amen.

Road Leading Into Eternity.

From everlasting to everlasting,
O' God, You are always there.

Your creation reflects Your majesty; Your Son
given unto man, showing that You really care.

Without You, O' Lord, humanity would
be totally lost!

The gift of Christ has been given to us—
yes, You have paid the cost!

Happy is the one created in the image of God.

Upon seeing Jesus, he receives Him and forever
becomes God's child!

Your grace, O' God, is sufficient to
save all of mankind!

Alas, why is it, that many eyes remain blind?

The road leading into Eternity,
strangely has two paths:

The broad path leads one into darkness;
the other leads one into a life that will always last.

Why, O' God, would You allow this to be?

God's answer: "I desire a people, in choosing
Jesus, will also be made free."

SECTION ONE:

ROAD LEADING INTO ETERNIY.

DEVOTION:

Jesus, the Only Way.

Jesus speaking to His disciples: "'Let not your hearts be troubled. Believe in GOD; believe also in Me. In My Father's house are many rooms. If it were not so, would I have told you that I go to prepare a place for you? And if I go and prepare a place for you, I will come again and will take you to Myself, that where I am you may be also. And you know the way to where I am going. Thomas said to Him, 'Lord, we do not know where You are going. How can we know the way?' Jesus said to him, 'I am the way, and the truth, and the life. No one comes to the Father except through Me.'" (John 14: 1-6 ESV).

<hr/>

Jesus made this claim to Thomas just before the Jewish leaders captured Him, the night when He was delivered into the hands of men living in darkness, tried, sentenced, and put on a cross. When Jesus had given up His life for us, it was for our redemption.

He did this out of His obedience to the Father. Because He paid the price, —all who place their trust in Him are now set free, forgiven of their sins, and allowed to live in the presence of God. You might ask, is Thomas's question valid? Is it also possible, because no man truly understands the transformation process, that God provides for His chosen?

Its stated in John 3:16, that "'For GOD so loved the world, that He gave His Only Son, that whoever believes in Him should not parish but have eternal life.'" (John 3:16 ESV): Therefore, it is because of God's love for mankind, that by our choosing to follow Jesus, we can be set free to live.

PRAYER: Heavenly Father, Thank You for giving us Your Son, so that we may have life and live it abundantly. Thank You for assuring us, that we can truly know the way home to You. As we are drawn to You, we begin to discover the real truth, as we learn to live unto Jesus Christ with humble gratitude. Indeed, we cherish Your precious name. Amen.

Understanding Eternity.

Eternity—how can a man truly understand?
His beginning is the result of God's hand,
As He created man in His own image.
The depth of God's creation is beyond a
man's imagination.

Can a man be guided toward Eternal life?
Or must he dwell forever in his selfish strife?
In running away from his Master, what is he
hoping to find?
As he runs from the light, seeking
to remain blind?

Can a man build his own earthly kingdom
and be satisfied?
Perhaps, for a moment, but soon after, he
will be fried.
The road toward death is broad and wide.
Can a man truly run from it to hide?

So, a man without faith in God's Appointed One,
His Begotten and Only Son
Who paid the price so that man may live
With God forever, enjoying the love He gives.
A man without faith will live in darkness,
Away from the Son of God and His kindness.

About Your Glory.

Allow me, O' God, to reflect upon Your glory;
For indeed, it tells a story.
It is a story about Your love for mankind,
A story which speaks of giving sight to all who
are blind.

By Your glory, all of creation has come into being.
And by Your grace, Your light shines upon the
worshipers to be seeing
How Your glory manifests itself into the
lives of men,
Freeing them from the bondage of their sin.

Your glory points to the cross
Where Your Son, the Son of God, saves the loss,
Redeeming them in His holy name.

Vessel of God's Love.

A long time ago, before our time,
God had a vision for His creation, mankind.
Creating a world that would know no sin,
And all who would enter His creation would
be welcomed in.

Thus, the marriage of holiness between
husband and wife,
Were designed by God, to never learn of strife.
Fellowship would come to be whole and pure,
The love that flowed, would by itself, be a
natural cure.

Mankind was set apart to be holy and free,
To create before God, a holy world for all of
creation to see.
But alas, the fallen angels had a different plan:
They came to destroy and ruin man.

So came the great fall of man from God's grace,
which destroyed the purity of the human race.
Lonely, and in despair, mankind fell away,
Not knowing if there would ever be
a renewed day.

Yet, God promised to redeem mankind
once again.
He sent Jesus Christ to become the atonement
for all human sin.
His death upon a cross,
Was viewed by many, a total waste and loss;
Yet, God was showing mankind of a better way.
Not understood by the worldly wise, not having
anything to say.

The resurrection of Jesus, restored the hope of
the fallen man,
That he will dwell in the house of the Lord, to
forever stand
In the presence of God, fully forgiven
and restored.
Knowing, although unworthy, he is redeemed
by the Lord.

Jesus went away, in order to send another,
A comforter, to bring together mankind, as sister
and brother.
Flowing from above,
Is God's love.
Filling HIS vessels to share the good news,
That God has given us new life and the
strength to choose,
A life, worth the living,
Of sharing and of giving.

God's Promises are Indeed Pure.

Pure are Your promises, O' Lord, that to us
You've given.
You've sent Your Son to live, to die, and
to be risen.
Pure is the salvation plan, as Jesus came to save,
Indeed, Christ paid the price, so that the path
can be paved.

How precious are Your promises given unto man;
If only, we, the wicked, could truly understand,
That we are being called to a holier place,
No matter who we are among the human race.

All you people, let us come now to sing
Praises to God, and our worship to bring
Forth before our Lord, for the promises He gave,
That leads us to His home, precious to Him, and
are saved.

Source of Liberation.

Lord Jesus, You are the source of man's liberation.
Your ministry among us is a true cause for
celebration!
You've healed the sick, brought sight to the blind,
Set the prisoner free, and gave Your life for all
of mankind.

What a treasure You've become to all who fix
their eyes upon You!
Your grace and mercy is ever so great, as we find
in You, all that is true.
You pour out Your blessings upon all
who love You.
You still seek after the lost, bringing them into
Your truth.

GOD, You Alone are Wise!

Infinite, Immortal, GOD, You alone are wise!
You've created the lands, the oceans, yes, even
the skies.
You are the Ruler of all that's upon the earth;
By raising up Your chosen people, You have given
them second birth.

Your infinite wisdom has caused all creation to be.
You provide for its existence, allowing it to be free.
Your loving kindness is felt throughout the land,
As You bid Your own to come before You
and stand.

As You cast away the sins of mankind,
You bring sight to the spiritually blind.
You raise up Your own, who once were dead,
Giving them the Bread of Life and Living Water,
so they may be well-fed.

Worthy is Our Creator and King.

Worthy is our GOD, Creator and King.
He has raised up a choir of worshipers to sing
Of His greatness and almighty hand!
Who, before Him, is worthy enough to stand?

He put into place the earth with its sky,
And through the air, do the clouds fly?
The sun gives the earth its warmth and glow,
Many rivers to the ocean, do flow.

He created Man in His own image to be,
True worshipers of His, living in His glory,
as beings set free.
Despite the fact that mankind had fallen
from grace—
He sent His Son to redeem the human race.

Christ will come again to rescue His own,
Bringing them forth to God's holy throne.
It is there that a feast will be made to
honor the bride,
As the groomsman takes her hand,
with love and pride.

For there shall come a new beginning,
Which will last forever, and there will
be no ending.

What a glorious Eternity that will be,
When all of creation will be made new, and
truly be free.

Grantor of Human Desire.

Blessed be to the God of Israel, the one and only
true light,
That shines upon His people, giving them
real sight.
He is the only true GOD, who is able to save His
chosen ones.
He lifts them up into positions of becoming His
daughters and sons.

Grantor of all human desire,
You have sheltered Your own from the darts of
Satan's fire.
On what ground can God's people boast, except
upon Jesus who claims
His own, rescuing them from their enemies,
who are deemed to be tossed into God's
judgment flames?

Grantor of joy to all who call upon His name,
He assures them that from age to age, He
is the same.
No greater love can His people find,
Than, when God sent His Son to save the lost, as
He brings sight to the blind.

Christt, Installed as King.

Why do nations insist on having wars?
What is it that causes people to want to score?
Aren't the nations aware that they are fighting
against the Lord?
He is able to pronounce judgment by the use of
His sword.

As leaders of the world seek to fight,
They are also taking aim at God, unaware, that
soon, they will be put to flight.
For Jesus Christ will soon return,
taking His stand
Against the wickedness of this world, and
claiming it as His land.

Call upon Jesus, and an inheritance you
shall find;
Yes, He will shine His light into the eyes of
the blind.
As for the wicked, they will flee from His sight;
And, out of fear, they will experience God's anger
and might.
Listen to the warnings that God gives:
You are to worship God and for Him
alone, to live.

For without accepting Christ as Lord of your life,
Can you truly expect to escape God's wrath by
your personal flight?

Happy is the man who finds refuge in
Jesus, the Lord.
Because he who lives by faith, and not by
sight or sword,
Moved, by the Holy Spirit, he follows in
Jesus's way,
Trusting that Jesus will take care of him
every day.

Free to Live.

Born again, into the Holy Spirit, we are now
free to live
In God's grace, empowered to live and to give.
One might ask: "How can this be?"
It is not by our own works that would cause us
to be free;
But rather, it is by God's design, through the
work of His Son.
Because, He is the Father's anointed one.

For as the Son of God died upon a cross for the
sins of mankind,
Found in the holy of holy, the veil torn, giving
sight to the blind.
In His imagery, God caused us to come to know,
That by gazing upon the Lamb, who hung
on a cross—
Man is now able to learn of God's way, never
again to be lost.

Thus, by having faith in Jesus Christ, we are
justified by God in His loving grace.
As He offers forgiveness to all who
seek His face—
The face of Jesus, who rose again, causing
resurrection to be.
Now, life in Christ, indeed has come, and
it is free!

May Your Glorious Name
Be Honored Forever!

Dear God, may Your name be glorified forever!
Let Your people before You sing.
Hallelujah to our great and wonderful King!
As we enter Your Kingdom—never,
No, never, allow us to be entertained by sin again.

May Your glorious name be forever honored
and praised!
May our voices before You be raised,
As we sing to You, with a sense of awe.
Thank You for Your Son,
For it is through Him, that the victory is won.
Jesus, You have rescued us from the fall.

Praise to You, God, the Father, Creator of
all things.
And to You, Lord Jesus, for the salvation that
You bring—
You paid the price to save us all.
Indeed, You have redeemed us from the fall.
And to You, O' Holy Spirit, the Giver of Peace,
You comfort us and have committed us to
the Father—
Our souls to experience release.

Embracing the Wind of God.

Is there a way for a man to embrace the
wind of God?
Do the words of this question seem to be
rather odd?
How does a man embrace the wind of God—
how can it come to be?
If a man could embrace God's wind, what
would he see?

The wind of God moves about us, as if it is
self-willed.
Can a man who feels the blowing of the Wind be
made to be still?
Long enough to empower that man's will?
At that moment, can that man embrace
God's wind?
Can there be a healing for that man, who is
guilty of sin?

Ah, YES! There is a way: It is through
God's Son;
He is God's anointed one!
It is through Him that a man is able to embrace
God's wind and forever live!
It is then that the wind of God embraces the
man, teaching him how to love and how to give.

Believer's Case Before God.

In the eyes of our holy God, we would be found
guilty, left to our own accord.
Because of our wicked ways, can God truly afford
To extend His grace to wicked men,
As they argue their case of righteousness, as they
before God stand?

However, God sees the believer in a
different light:
Shining, like the sun, the soul is made bright;
He sees there, in the depth of the soul,
A trusting faith, that makes the soul whole.

The believer makes his case, as he gazes upon
God's Son,
Acknowledging Him, to be the true and
anointed One.
By shedding the blood of life for the sake
of mankind,
To the repentant sinner, his soul to God,
does bind.
The case is made by the believer's response
When he receives the Savior—he is
cleansed at once!
He is made whole, in the likeness of God.
He becomes a child of His, as throughout
Eternity, he does trod.

Do You Believe?

Do you believe in the one true God, who created
the heavens and the earth?
Do you believe in the one true God, who gave
His Son to die upon a cross for the forgiveness of
your sins?
Do you believe in the One True God, who offers
you Eternal life that will never end?

He is the Author of LIFE,
The Ancient of Days,
Revealing Himself to us despite the darkness
and strife;
Causing us to draw near to Him with a heart full
of praise.
Beautiful words He has spoken in His
Book of love,
Raising the soul of man to seek after the
things above.
Perhaps you would ask: "How can this be?"
Answer: He created you for His purposes and to
set you free.

When the Soul Steps Out of Condemnation.

Oh, hardened heart of the soul who refuses
to believe
In the Son of God, and opening his arms
to receive;
Is it because your pride and arrogance has come
in the way,
Of you seeing God's grace and mercy as He
works upon your soul today?

There is no condemnation for the soul that
comes to believe
In Jesus Christ, seeking Him into the soul's heart
to receive.
O', closed-minded soul, are you bold enough to
open your eyes to see
The reality of your condition, and the need to
be set free?

Upon acknowledging the condition of your soul,
Repent, and seek to be made whole.
O' soul, you will be stepping out of
condemnation, to be set free,
To live out God's purpose for you as HE allows
you to be.

A Desire to Be Found.

Lord, I desire to be found in You.
Longing to come into You, as I give my life to
living for You.
I seek to be identified with You in your suffering
and also in your resurrection.
Empower me to live in your righteousness that
You have freely given to me.
As I call You, Lord, teach me how to obey.
Let my heart be submitted to You as I daily walk
in Your ways.

Thank You for being the Savior that You
are to me.
As I survey the cross, I come to know the cost
That You paid for my soul,
Causing in me the desire to be made whole.

In Receiving the Living Faith.

Soul, do you know what it takes to receive a
living faith?
On your part, O' Soul, what does it take?
Being born again, did you say?
Truly, without the Spirit coming into me, I would
never find the way.

Soul, how then do I receive the Holy Spirit, that
now lives in me?
Is it by first repenting, that causes me to be free?
Or is it by God, convicting me from within
In order for me to see the magnitude of
my own sin?

Soul, how did it come about that I've been saved?
Did Jesus pay the price for salvation's road
to be paved?
Look at the cross, and observe the Son of
man there:
He suffered and died for us because of God's love,
compassion, and care.

He bodily rose again to forever end death's sting.
So, as I behold the Messiah dying upon a cross,
Acknowledging Him, as such: No longer, O' Soul,
are you at a loss.
For all of mankind can now, as I, enter God's
Kingdom as a new creature, yes! As a new being.

Parable of the Unsaved Man.

This is a parable of the unsaved man:
He is the one who builds his home on
shifting sand;
Unaware, that he cannot save himself by the
works of his own hand,
As he looks upon his own image of a
promised land.

He works hard at becoming self-righteous in
his own eyes,
As he searches for God, up in the skies,
Telling Him there:"I found a way to be
pleasing to You,
By earning salvation by works as I seek to find
what I believe to be true!"

God replies to the unsaved man:"O man, do
you not see,
That by your own effort, finding true life, will
never come to be?
Only through the redemptive work of the
Son of man,
Can one be saved, by grace through faith, and be
brought forth to the Savior's hand?
Know that Jesus, the Messiah, is the Son of God
and the Son of man."

SECTION TWO:

REVELATION SONG!

DEVOTION:

Come and Drink from the Water of Life!

In the last chapter of Revelation, it says: "Blessed are those who wash their robes, so that they may have the right to the tree of life and that they may enter the city by the gates. Outside are the dogs and sorcerers and the sexually immoral and murderers and idolaters and everyone who loves and practices falsehood.

'I, Jesus, have sent my angel to testify to you about these things for the churches. I am the root and the descendant of David, the bright morning star.'

The Spirit and the Bride say, 'Come.' And let the one who hears say, 'Come.' And let the one who is thirsty come, let the one who desires take the water of life without price." (Rev. 22: 14-17 ESV).

Do you hear the calling of Jesus, bidding you to come and partake in the drinking from the well of living water? Indeed, it is the water of life. By partaking in it, it springs up as a living well from the soul.

Come and receive the Son of God and fellowship with Him. He is the King! Lord of our lives, and the Groom of the Church—His bride!

Let us sing praises to the King of kings, and the Lord of lords! He rules over us with love and grace. He is the Redeemer of the human race. And for those who boldly seek Him, He will embrace as His own.

———

PRAYER: Dear Lord Jesus, come soon. Bring Your people home. Let us forever bask in Your live and grace. In Your precious name. Amen.

Jesus Is the Beginning, Is the Now, And Is the Ending.

Lord Jesus, You are the beginning, and You are
the ending, and You are now.
May the words of Your mouth echo forever in my
life and show me how,
To best serve You in this world and in the next,
with love and cheerfulness.
Let my hands be to others a reflection of Your
loving-kindness.

Forgive Us Lord, For Leaving Our First Love.

Forgive us, Lord, for leaving our first love.
Just as the Holy Spirit had descended upon us
like a peaceful dove,
We were given the gift of Eternal life.
No longer do we need to set our minds on our
personal strife.

Once again, Lord, come light our hearts with
Your fire and grace!
Give to us again, the boldness to share Your love
to all of the human race.
Let us once again sing praises to You, Lord above.
Let us embrace one another in Christian love.

Behold, I Stand.

Behold I, the Lord, Jesus Christ stand.
I am knocking at the door of all the people living
in the land.
I desire to fellowship and to give new meaning to
your name.
I am the beginning and the end; forever, I
remain the same.

Soon, I will come to take my people away.
Those who do not know Me won't know
what to say.
I am the living water, yes, I am the pillar of life.
Come to me and repent, then I will heal you
from your sin and strife.

Singing A New Song

I'm singing a new song, Lord Jesus, about
Your grace.
Praise, hallelujah, and honor to the One, who
redeemed the human race!
I come before Your throne, singing a new song.
Thank You, Jesus, for allowing me to belong.

Glory Hallelujah! Let my voice be raised.
Glory Hallelujah, let my new song give
You praise!
In singing this song, may it reflect Your story.
And, as the words of praise leave my mouth, may
it bring to You glory?

I'm singing a new song, Lord Jesus, about Your
loving kindness.
Praise, hallelujah, and honor to the One who has
ended man's blindness.
Coming before Your throne, I give myself to
You to own.
Thank You, Lord Jesus, for reaping the harvest of
that which You've sown.

Glory hallelujah, let my voice be raised.
Glory hallelujah, let my new song give You praise.
In singing this song, may it reflect Your story.

And as the words of praise leave my mouth, may
it bring You glory?

I'm singing to You, Lord Jesus, about Your
coming Kingdom.
Praise, hallelujah, and honor to the One who
gives Your people freedom
To choose to follow You, and by Your grace,
be set free
To sing Your new song from now on throughout
all of Eternity.

Glory hallelujah, let my voice be raised!
Glory hallelujah, let my new song give You praise.
In singing this new song, may it reflect Your story,
And as the words of praise leave my mouth, may
it bring You glory?

Worthy Are You, O' Lord, Our God.

Worthy are You, O' Lord, our God.
It is You who created all things at Your will.
Worthy are You, O' Lord, our God.
It is You who governs with strength, despite Your
voice being gentle and still.

Worthy are You, O' Lord, our God,
For You have made us purposely to give You glory.
Worthy are You, O' Lord, our God,
For all that You have made tells us a great story.

Worthy Is God's Holy Lamb.

Who, in all of God's creation, is worthy to open
the seven-sealed book?
Who, in God's creation, deserves to break its
seals and take a look?
BEHOLD! The Lion of Judah, it is He, who
visits man as a sacrificial Lamb.
He alone is worthy. For it is He who redeemed
those who dwell in the earth's land!

Worthy are You, Lord Jesus. For You have given
mankind the privilege of having new life
Worthy are You, Lord Jesus, for You have given
mankind the power to walk away from strife.
You, Lord Jesus, have been slain for many, though,
those who do come are few.
Will You open up the seals from the book? —
Will You do it now, so that all of mankind can
come to see and, of it, preview?

A Kingdom of priests, You have made.
As the glitter of the earth begins to fade.
The new earth is about to come and take its place.
A new world is about to come to house the
redeemed human race.

We ask, as You sit upon the throne of time, to tell
us of Your story,

Of how You defeated death's sting and bought us
for fellowship and Your glory.
Indeed, to the world, You are its light,
Given unto mankind, granting them
spiritual sight.

Coming of the Great Tribulation.

Listen carefully, all you saints, as the day of great
sorrow draws near.
Many will come, claiming to be the light, yet they
will rule by fear.
Can you hear now the sounds that tell of the
troubles that lie ahead?
Indeed, the time is coming where many will have
their blood shed.

As food becomes too expensive to buy,
Many, through starvation, will be destined to die.
Will there be anyone, who will come to
save the day?
Alas, a time of darkness will fall, and of its terror,
who will be left to say?

Many a saint, will beg Christ to deliver. But He
will say: "Wait."
Satan and his followers will stir the souls of
mankind, causing them to want and to hate.
But this too, will soon pass away.
Jesus is coming to make ready a new and
glorious day.

Robes Made of White.

As the Great Tribulation ravaged the land,
Many suffered and were no longer able to stand.
Behold! There is something to see.
A great multitude, wearing white robes, how
can this be?
The blood of Jesus had come over the land.
He has washed their robes with His hand.
Making clean the multitude who once were dead,
Bringing the forth to feed upon the living bread.

As He gathers them together, He leads
them away,
To where there is living water, where they are
able to drink their fill every day.
Holy are the ones who trust in the Lord,
For they will escape the wrath of God's
judging sword.

Marriage Feast of the Lamb.

BEHOLD! The MASTER has just laid
out a feast,
For the souls of the earth, that from death
has released.
The trumping is sounding in the air,
Giving away to a rapture of the saints to
meet Jesus there.

The marriage and the feast is about to begin,
As the Tribulation brings the old earth order
to an end.
As the Bride of Christ looks upon Jesus with joy,
Sounds of music and singing, brought forth a
great noise.

"BEHOLD!" The MASTER said,
"The marriage of the bride and the Son.
He is My Anointed One.
You are now His people in His Kingdom.
Though He rules with an iron arm, He grants
His people with a great deal of freedom.
"Come forth now in celebration,
And, as sounds of pain rumble on, in the
Great Tribulation,
Come forth to the feast that is laid,
In celebration of the price, My Son, for you
had paid."

When The Earth Is Damaged.

As Christ revealed before John's face,
He pondered upon the thought of the seventh
seal as it was broken, and what it would do to
the entire human race.

Christ called, "Come with Me and
listen to the sounds that I hear.
For behold, they are getting louder as we
draw near."

Listen to the saints, of the tribulation and,
prayers, as they are lifted up to Me.
And behold, the image there, is it coming like
a judgment sword?
Could the smoke of incense, that you smell,
be getting in the way,
Mankind's hurried schedules, as they make a
living every day?"

As John heard the first trumpet call, what
did he see?
A volcano erupting, taking out many a tree.
The fire of its fury spread throughout the land,
Spreading its might as far as the ocean sand.

As John heard the second trumpet call,
what did he see?

At a distance, he saw a great mountain explode
and was cast to the ground,
Polluting the waters of the nearby sea,
Filling it with debris.

When the third trumpet sounded,
One third of the creatures were no longer there.
Did mankind truly care?
The economy of mankind had taken a great spill
Many still wondered what caused such
a great kill?

Then John saw a star falling upon the earth,
And wondered, *could this make for an evil
second birth?*
A birth to a death which is bitter and
full of dread,
Causing many to die, and creating a situation
where many a man ceases to be fed?

When John heard the fourth trumpet, he looked
up at the sky,
Observing a great massive cloud, floating above
the earth very high.
As he wondered, *what caused this cloud to over
the earth spread?*
It appeared that it was taking away the earth's
ability to make life's bread.

John asked, "What is to come, now that
the damage is done?
As I gaze upon the earth, I find that
everything is gone.
Is there any place to hide?
Do the people go into buildings or do they
stay outside?"

The Pit and the River.

As John heard another sound, he asked,
"Is this something to fear?"
Scorpions, by the millions, were
coming out of a pit.
The scorpions scattered there and here.
As the fifth trumpet sounded, it announced the
coming of misery, placing mankind into
a terrible fit.

As the sixth trumpet sounded, John looked upon
a river, which faced East.
He saw an army, two hundred million horses and
soldiers, marching to kill
A third of mankind, enjoying the immoral feast.
Where can a person hide from such a wrath?
Where can they go to find peace and be still?

A Sweet Little Book,
Made Bitter.

One day a book was given to John to see.
The messenger encouraged him to taste it, and
of it eat.
John's tongue found it to be very sweet.
The first impression of the book made him think
it was a treat.
The content of the words spoken there,
Had both a warning and compassionate care.

As John digested the book,
His stomach felt a bitter taste, and full of pain,
That's when he discovered and found,
That without the Lord of Light, there was for
mankind no hope and no gain.

Two Witnesses.

In the darkest hours of the Tribulation,
Came two witnesses with a revelation.
They shared with the people of the Lord's way,
But the unrepentant refused to listen
to what they had to say.

For forty-two months, did the witnesses speak,
A few did come before them, and they were
touched with God's light.
But woe to those who failed to listen, and before
God, became meek,
For they are destined to be banished
from God's sight.

Death came to the witnesses,
as darkness did arise,
The beast of the Devil will attack them
from the skies.
For three and a half days, the witnesses lay dead,
To be seen by the world, who celebrated, feasted,
and became well-fed.

As the seventh trumpet sounded,
a joyous sound filled the air!
The Lord, Jesus Christ, returned,
as the men of darkness stare.

He establishes His Kingdom and
puts to an end,
All of man's evilness, all of man's sin.

The wicked gasped and became distraught,
For it wasn't the Lord that they sought.
Judgment day had come upon mankind,
Exposing the spiritually-gifted and the
spiritually-blind.

A Beacon, a Deceiver, a Redeemer, and His Army.

John saw an amazing sight that appeared in
the skies:
A Beacon, a Deceiver, the Redeemer, and His
army appeared on high.
The Beacon gave birth to a Redeeming Child,
Who came into the world to rule with a rod. Yet,
He was gentle and mild.
The Deceiver raged with anger, as he went after
the Chosen Light,
Which caused a war to break out between God's
army and the Deceiver.
Overpowered, the Deceiver was cast away,
Being blocked from ever seeing the light of day.

Day of Salvation.

The day of salvation is finally here,
No longer do the redeemed need to fear.
Because the healing has come to those who
love the Lord.
As for the deceiver and his followers, they have
been cut down by the sword.

The blood of the Redeemer has redeemed for
Himself, a new race.
For those who have come to depend upon Him,
comes now, into His living grace.
No more tears of sorrow will ever again enter
their hearts.
And, as for the deceiver, he will be swept away
by God's piercing darts.

Woe to the earth, as it faces its last day,
The deceiver will attempt to draw many from
God's way.
Out of anger and wrath, he will come to
destroy the earth,
Preventing as many as he can, from receiving
God's spiritual birth.

A War of Rage.

The deceiver, in anger, wages a war.
Determined through the battle, to even the score.
He seeks to destroy the sons and daughters
of the Light,
He casts a spell and hopes to put the
truth out of sight.

But his time is short,
And the army of God, so very strong,
How can the Devil truly retort?
Thus, the Lord, once and for all, defeated
all that was wrong.

Many, who knew Jesus, came to testify,
And many witnessed the miracle of new life, by
Seeing the blood of the Lamb as He
redeemed His own.

Casting away evil, as if it were a stone.
No more anger, no more strife.
Jesus is now here to give second life.
For the judgment has come to judge the wrong.
And healing has come to cause the sons of Light
to sing a new song.

Image of the Beast.

What happened to earth on that dark, dreary day,
When Satan was in control and having his way?
Alas, a beast had come out of the sea,
Offering to the world's people a way to peace and
become free.

It appeared to the world that this beast was kind.
Because of his deception, the world became
spiritually blind.
Given authority, he ran man's affairs,
Because of man's pride, God cast away this
people to tend to their cares.

Another beast came upon the land.
This beast declared the beast of the sea, to be
really grand.
He required of man to make an image of the
wounded beast,
And to bow down before it to worship and feast.

Suddenly, the image of the beast came alive!
He caused the people of the world to be deprived
Of knowing God and His amazing nature
and grace.
It is at this point, that spiritual darkness
overcame the human race.

Who is this image of the beast,
Coming into its own glory, causing people to
worship it and, before it, feast?
This beast of image is able to tear out of men, the
desire to learn of God and of His ways,
Casting a shadow, which darkens the day.

The road of life that the image made did appear
to be smooth and well-paved.
Yet, he robbed from many any hope of ever
being saved,
By the blood of Jesus, which paid for us all;
Even now, can a man see that he must be saved
from this deadly fall?

Perseverance of the Redeemed.

As time drew to a close, the end in sight,
Who will be able to escape God's wrath, ending
human blight?
The first fruits of God will lead the way
For the redeemed to be released on
Judgment Day.

It is because the perseverance of the Redeemed
brought them through the darkness into the light.
Rejoicing now in Jesus, because they've been
given a vision to see God's holy might.

Alas, to those who remain in the dark to dwell.
The fire of destruction is coming to cast them
into Hell.
For the wrath of the Lord draws ever so near,
That the unredeemed truly need to fear.

Singing On the Sea of Glass.

John saw a new vision; it became very clear.
He saw many men and women, victorious over
their fear.
As before God, they came upon the Sea of
Glass singing.
For they have witnessed the final wrath of God,
which angels were bringing.

As the people stood before the Lord, they were
declared holy and right,
Because they overcame the influence of
Satan's might.
They sang the songs of Moses and of the Lamb,
In the presence of God, they felt the peace and
warmth that surrounded them.

They sang, "Great is the LORD, He alone is
worthy of praise.
Hear, oh hear, our voices that we raise.
True is the Lord, in all of His ways.
He rules with an iron hand, all of His days,
Which will never end,
Now and forever, Eternity begins.
Who is like Him, holy and true?
O' God, we bring all of our praise to You.

"For those who love the Lord, will into God find,
A release from sin, and the effects of being blind.
Who can stand before the Lord and not fear?
Holy and righteous is He, yet, His compassion
draws us near.
He is a marvelous God indeed!
HE provides for man's spirit, yea, for man's soul,
HE feeds."

These are the words John heard them sing,
As he prayed for God to bring
Home, those who long to be,
Forever into the Lord Jesus, made forever free.

God's Bowls of Wrath.

John sees another vision, pertaining to the end,
Causing him to ask himself, "What do I
really see?"
John is seeing the final judgment upon mankind,
forcing evil to depart.
He is now seeing the Second Coming of Jesus
Christ, to set His people free.

What came forth are God's bowls of wrath,
poured to cause pain,
To those who hated the Lord.
For it is out of lust, that evil men desire to gain.
Alas for them, they will be slaughtered
by the sword.

The first bowl of wrath brought about sores,
Upon those who have the mark of the beast.
They are the ones who refused to listen to God
in finding open doors.
Instead, they scoffed at the Anointed One,
who came for them, to release.

The second bowl of wrath turned water
into blood.
It killed all the life found in the sea.
It appeared, to those who witnessed it, like a red,
gushing flood.
It frightened them sorely, causing them to flee.

The third bowl of wrath also changed water
into blood,
All the rivers and streams about.
It appeared to have caused a red flood.
Declared an angel of God: "God is just to find
the sins of mankind out."

The fourth bowl of wrath caused the sun to give
extreme heat.
Rays of great intensity fell upon the earth.
It caused human flesh to burn like cooked meat.
It caused great pain as human skin deeply hurt.

The fifth bowl of wrath fell upon the beast.
It caused a darkness to fall.
No longer can the sons of darkness feast.
Yet, in spite of their pain, they refused to repent
or to hear God's call.

The sixth bowl of wrath fell and caused a stir
among the hearts of men, and a desire to fight.
Thus, the armies of the world came out to meet
on Armageddon's field,
declaring themselves as having the right,
To live as they wish, and refusing of their
wishes to yield.

The seventh bowl of wrath created a lightning
for all to see.

The earth now poured out its fire, as it trembled
and quaked.
The earth's destructive force left no city to be,
Concludes the judgment as the earth ends
its shake.

No island could be seen, no one was there to care.
For the volcanoes and earthquakes brought an
end to it all.
No man was alive to open their arms to share,
Because man refused to listen to God's
pleading call.

Shocked as John was, he asked of God, "What
sense does it make,
For men to turn away
From You, O' God, and Your glory, and of
You to forsake
The grace that You offer them every day?

"Sorrow has come, O' Lord, but who is to blame?
Is not the God of Israel our Redeemer to be?
Yes, Lord, from age to age, You remain the same.
If only we would turn our hearts to You and see."

The Beast and the Lamb.

Living in the world during the last days, there
was a beast, who, to many, appeared to be grand.
Ah, but before the Lord, soon he would
not stand.
Though he duped the world into believing that
he was the way
To find security, pleasure, and happiness, in
living each day.

A Lamb came into the world years ago to save
Sinners from destruction. He offered mankind a
better way
For the lost. Yet, many didn't recognize Him as
the Son of light.
Therefore, they went about their worldly ways,
keeping Him out of sight.

A war raged on that last day,
When the beast charged against Jesus, as
witnesses stood in dismay.
For the beast was destroyed, and everything
appeared to be lost.
They failed to recognize that Jesus paid the price
for man's sin, paying the cost.

An end of wickedness is surely to be.
A time will be granted for those who seek the
Lord and made free,
Where darkness will be no more,
And God will never keep score.

Where Did the Great City of Babylon Go?

Where did the great city of Babylon go?
It was once a city of splendor, now it's a
city of woe.
Where was that great city that sat upon
many a hill,
When voices were once heard, but now in silence,
was still.

If only the people could see the reasons why,
Babylon was destroyed, and its legacy had
passed by.
Perhaps they would see the inequities of
their own ways,
And would have repented, choosing to live for
Jesus, the rest of their days.

Second Coming.

As the deception of the world held,
on the horizon, what did John see?
The Lord, Jesus Christ, on a white horse,
coming to set His people free.
The battle lines drawn, and death bringing a
gloom of fear.
Many of the wicked are forever destroyed,
because they didn't listen, nor did they hear,
Of the message of salvation, so rich and pure,
That, to those who came to its light, found
themselves cured
Of the blight that had entered in
Their souls which caused them to sin.
The scrolls were opened, the Book of
Life appeared,
Judgment had fallen, as their eyes turned
to God, in fear.
They knew that their doom was sure,
Because they failed to live a life in Jesus,
declared holy and pure.

Who will be in that Book of Life?
Who will look upon Jesus, who redeems man
from their strife?
Who will repent of their evil ways to give
their lives in following Jesus's ways?

When they stand before Jesus,
what will they say?

To be declared righteous, before God,
one must have faith.
He needs to recognize, that by himself,
he can't get rid of all selfishness and hate.
Only on bended knee, before Jesus
with a repented heart,
Can a believer find the gift of salvation
and life, and of God, become a part
Of His new creation, that He put into the
redeemed man's life;
Free from corruption, sin, and strife.

As the vision passed by, John fell upon his knee,
And before God, he did plea:
"Come, Jesus, please come again.
Remove forever from man's heart the
desire for him to sin.
AMEN."

Thousand Year Reign.

Judgment of the earth is over and done;
The deceptive powers of Satan are totally gone.
The first resurrection is now complete,
The dragon and the false prophet went down
in defeat.

John asked the Lord, "How long, this time,
will You be?"
Jesus said, "A thousand years is to pass by,
The spirit of mankind will soar and fly,
Fulfilling the commission of how mankind
ought to be,
Yet, the time is limited for man to see.

"It isn't for mankind to know all the
mysteries of God,
Which, from man's perspective, seems to be odd.
Alas, a time will come again,
When deception will creep in, and sin will
again enter in.

"It is then that the Final Battle will come.
To bring to an end spiritual darkness,
And to usher in a new and an Eternal Kingdom.
It will be there that God will shine HIS
loving-kindness.

"Thus, into the Lake of Fire, will the
rebellious ones go,
Banished from God, sent into Eternal woe."
At this point, the second death has arrived for all
unregenerated beings,
Because of their blindness, they didn't see the gift
of life that God did bring.

On that final day, God stood up to speak,
In His words, He called out the arrogant, and
He called out the meek.
The heavens and earth had passed away.
There came the final judgment on this
dreadful day.

Book of Life.

The Book of Life just appeared.
Those who only knew of darkness trembled
and feared,
That upon God's calling, they may never hear
their name.
For He is GOD, and forever,
He remains the same.

Out of their fear and out of their hate,
They came to realize that it was too late,
To make amends with God for their wicked ways.
Now, they are sentenced to Eternal torment for
the rest of their days,
And will live in a cycle of torment, which will
never end.
Because they rejected Christ and
chose to live in sin.

For the names that appeared in the Book of Life,
There were no more tears, and no more strife.
A wonderful joy brought about a peace of mind.
They found themselves in a community full of
love, and kind.

Love was the key that held them
close to the Lord.
No longer was there a need for a sword.

Peace had come, guided by God's light,
As they lived with God, with the darkness
out of sight.

No one thirst, in that promised land.
Behold, their numbers—, they numbered more
than the sands.
I personally asked the Lord Jesus, "How
can this be?"
He answered—"Come now, Bill, just follow Me."

All Things Made New.

There came into being, a new Heaven and a
new earth.
God now lives with and gives spiritual birth
To a paradise of glory and fame,
To which there is no end, and all of the new
creation remains the same.

Difficult it is, for the mind's eye to see,
How God will grant man, a new world in which
he can be free.
Living in a world where God is honored
and praised,
With a new song to be sung, with voices raised.

No longer will the creatures of God be motivated
by selfishness and greed.
For the Lord only will they worship, and to His
will, they will heed.
Great is the day when Heaven and earth
will combine,
For all who are saved to live forever, being kind.

For Redeemed, the Tree of Life.

Happy is the repented sinner whose robes were
washed clean,
For theirs is the Tree of Life.
Happy is the child of God, who, upon Jesus
Christ, he does lean,
For God will remove his personal strife.

Indeed, the Lord, Jesus Christ, is coming soon!
Like a thief, He may appear in the night or
during the day.
As Jesus knocks at your door, He asks of you:
"Do you have room for me, to be in your heart?
Will you have supper with Me, and of Me declare
allegiance, and never from Me depart?"

Singing About Grace.

I'm singing a new song, Lord Jesus, about grace.
Praise, hallelujah, and honor to the One who
redeemed the human race.
I come before Your throne, singing a new song.
Thank You, Jesus, for allowing me to belong.

Glory hallelujah, let my voice be raised!
Glory hallelujah, may my new song bring
You praise!
As I sing this new song, may it reflect Your story.
As the words of praise leave my mouth, may the
words bring You glory.

I'm singing a new song, Lord Jesus, about Your
loving kindness,
Praise, hallelujah, and honor to the One who
ended man's blindness.
Coming before Your throne, I give myself to
You to own.
Thank You, Jesus, for reaping the harvest You
have sown.

Glory hallelujah, let my voice be raised!
Glory hallelujah, may my new song bring
You praise!
As I sing this new song, may it reflect Your story.

As the words of praise leaves my mouth, may
the words bring You glory.

I'm singing to You, Lord Jesus, about
Your coming Kingdom.
Praise, hallelujah, and honor, to the One
who gives us freedom
To choose to follow You and to be forever set free,
To forever sing Your new song from now into
all of Eternity.

Glory hallelujah, let my voice be raised!
Glory hallelujah, may my new song bring
You praise!
As I sing this new song, may it reflect Your story,
As the words of praise leave my mouth, may the
words bring You glory?

SECTION THREE

IN LIVING FOR JESUS.

Devotion- Shine Your Light into The World.

Reading from the Book of Matthew, Jesus said to His followers: "'You are the light of the world.—A city set on a hill cannot be hidden.—Nor do people light a lamp and put it under a basket, but on a stand, and it gives light to all in the house. —In the same way, let your light shine before others, so that they may see your good works and give glory to your Father, who is in heaven." (Matt. 5: 14-16 ESV).

As believers in Christ, did we not come to faith by others who have walked in the faith before us? Likewise, we too must shine our light in such a way that the Holy Spirit can work through us, pointing others to come into a saving faith in Christ Jesus, as did we.

PRAYER: Father, thank You for Your Son, who has given us new life. By the power of Your Holy Spirit, allow our faith to shine upon others, so that they too, can have what we have in You—salvation! In Jesus's name. Amen.

O' Lord, When Is It Time?

O' Lord, when is it time to live,
To share life's story, as one learns to give?
O' Lord, when is it time to love,
Sharing our time and affection, as we gaze to
You above?

O' Lord, when is it time for Your peace,
Which causes to forgive others, and of their
sins, release?
O' Lord, when is it time for Your grace,
As we, Your followers, extend mercy and justice
to the human race?

The Shepherd Cares For Me.

As I bask in the presence of my Shepherd, what
does my heart see?
A God who always cares for me.
He is the Provider of all my needs, and He
gives me rest.
He soothes my overwhelming fears and brings
peace to my heart, which is found restless.

By His healing power, He makes me whole again.
By His convicting command, He turns my
heart from sin.
By His grace, I walk upon the road of life.
By His mercy, I find myself in His righteousness
and truth, as He leads me out of strife.

How great a God is He?
Who, by His loving-kindness, has set me free,
To live forever unto Him, throughout Eternity,
And forever allowing me to be.

Praises to the Lord.

Walking life's road with Jesus,
I find Him to be food for my soul.
He picks up all the pieces
Of my life, to make me whole.
He is true to His promises,
Watching me every day,
Guiding me down life's path,
Leading me on the narrow way.

I sing praises to the Lord,
He is worthy of my prayer.
He reaches out to touch me,
Because He truly cares.

He has called me to share the good news
Of His wonderful saving grace.
He longs to touch the lives of everyone,
And He came to redeem the human race.
What a privilege it is to be,
A follower of God's only Son.
It is because of His resurrection from death,
That life's victory has been won.

I sing praises to the Lord,
He is worthy of my prayer.
He reaches out to touch me,
Because He truly cares.

When Christ comes back again,
He will come back for me, as if a breath of wind.
He will wipe away my human tears.
He will put behind Him, all of my sins.
The redeemed human race will truly find joy,
For we will be brought home to God,
And, on that day, we will be pleasure in His sight.
We will see Him face-to-face.

I sing my praises to the Lord,
He is worthy of my prayer.
He reaches out to touch me,
Because He truly cares.

Father God, Draw Us Closer to You.

Father God, draw us closer to You.
Be to us, a safe haven, in the presence of
Your love.
Instill in us, a heart that is for You alone.
As we make our journey through life, yearning
to come home.

Let not our troubled hearts get in the way,
Of worshiping You every day.
Encourage us to grow in our faith,
So that our confidence is found in Your
work in us.

With gratitude, we come before You.
With thanksgiving for all that You do for us.
As You provide
For our needs every day, bring us Your prosperity.
Let us walk into You in stride.
Be, forever, to us a guiding hand,
So that we will stand before You on that
great day,
As we hear YOUR voice speaking to us:
"Well done, good and faithful servant."

A Thanksgiving Poem

No greater God could there ever be,
Than our God, who has
set us free.
No greater grace could ever be poured,
To redeem us, as we call Him, Lord.
How can we in our hearts, give Him
thanksgiving,
For the opportunity He granted us for living?

Consider the stars and the sun of the sky,
The clouds above, and the birds that fly;
No better perfection, could God ever have made,
As the foundations of the earth, which
God has laid.
What glories can we avail to our
Heavenly Maker?
Who is more than our earthly Caregiver?

Our God has reached out to mankind in
many ways.
To be our King, throughout Eternity and a day,
And through His Son, He has given us life,
Freeing us from His wrath and from our
personal strife.
What greater love could our God ever show
Than to give a part of Himself to make us whole?

The things we have here on earth,
Before time, were all known to God, before
our birth.
The blessings and curses of our lives, in
which we bear,
Were always known to God, because He was
always there.
What greater truth could there ever be,
Than that God gives us new life, through His
Son, so that we may be made free?

We offer up this poem of thanksgiving, O' Lord,
As we sing praises to You, in one accord.

When Meeting the LORD.

Growing up in a home where we all knew that
God exists,
But afraid to believe that God, for us, would
truly enlist
Our names in life's Eternal Holy Book,
That gives us new life, opening our eyes toward
God, for a better look.

Not knowing God in a personal way,
We become vulnerable to life's influences, causing
us to go astray,
In beliefs that are not real, nor are they true;
Confusing us in our lives, causing us to feel blue.

My life before meeting the Lord,
Was a life which had very little direction, indeed,
I was bored.
I sought satisfaction through obtaining an
education,
Discovering that I did not know how to handle
life's frustrations.

When meeting the Lord Jesus, in a personal way,
I found a new meaning in my life, as I
lived each day.
Believing now that I am forever saved,

Which is based on my faith, and not on how
well I behave.

I walk in the Lord, in my personal life,
God made to know that I belong to Him, even in
my struggles and strife.
Convicting me of all of my wrong doings,
HE leads me into a righteous path, a path
worth pursuing.
I find my life in Christ to be full of joy and peace.
Living forever in Christ is an Eternal feast.

Kingdoms.

How are kingdoms impressed upon our minds?
As I reflect upon this theme, I have discovered
that there are many kinds.
How do I venture to list them all,
Spanning the time from the present to the fall?

Kingdoms of darkness seek to put to death,
All that's created from God's holy breath.
Worldly kingdoms are designed to enslave all
of mankind,
Robbing them of truth and leaving them
spiritually blind.

Kingdoms of the states often are led by
leaders of hate,
Insisting that his subjects look upon him and
appreciate.
Religious kingdoms that force their doctrines
upon others,
Fail to address the needs of all sisters
and brothers.

Kingdoms of men, who are very proud,
Brag of their good work as they speak out loud.
Kingdoms of the heart, yearn to divide
People from one another, in order to exalt
their pride.

Kingdoms that worship power grasp as much
as they can,
Ignoring the reality, that one day before GOD,
they will stand.
Kingdoms of the glands, seek after
pleasure and lust,
They rush through life empty, before they turn
back to dust.

Kingdoms of children, living inside their dreams,
Having fantasies of their world, dreaming up
adventurous schemes.
The kingdoms of leaders, who, of themselves,
they try to impress.
Will they ever understand that nothing in this
world will last?

Ah, but there is a Kingdom that is holy
and bright,
Given unto man, so that he may come to
the light.
It is not of this world, so that it can be displayed,
And as the forces of darkness look upon it, they
are utterly dismayed.

For this Kingdom will forever last,
And for those who seek after it, their lives into it,
they will cast.
Trusting in the Lamb that was slain and
rose again,

Will bring the redeemed into a Kingdom of
everlasting life.
They will leave behind all the other kingdoms
of strife.

There is Hope for the Righteous.

As the darkness falls upon mankind,
The human race is quickly becoming blind.
Is there any hope for the righteous?
Will light be given them to see?

As the forces of destruction bring forth an end,
In despair, the human race asks, "Will the good
life ever return again?"
For the righteous, living in this time,
Is there any hope to be found? Will they
be set free?

As darkness arises, and the righteous in Christ
place their faith,
Will they find peace in the midst of darkness?
Will they be able to live in Christ, and also be?

Yes, there is hope for the righteous, for they have
been found,
By God to be in the truth, their faith planted in
solid ground.
There is hope in the darkness, for those who seek
To be found in God, justified, and set free.

Showing Boldness in the Dark.

As I dwell among those living in darkness,
You are there to teach me how to act in kindness
Toward those who do not follow You.
Lord, teach them that indeed, You are true.
Truth comes by understanding the heart
of Your way;
Acknowledging You as God, as I live each day.
I find You near to me, even in the dark,
As my eyes turns to You in sharp focus.

I sense Your protection as You watch over me,
And, because of Your guidance, I am able to see
Your work and also Your glory,
As human life plays out Your story.

What Happens, When....?

What happens when the faithless pass away?
When their hopes and expectations no longer
hold sway?
It vanishes with them, as they lay in the grave,
No longer able to hear the Voice, that to them
would save.

What happens when those who are justified by
faith through God's grace,
Become prosperous in a city, which dwells
many-a-face?
Their blessing on the city causes them to
celebrate.
While the words of the wicked express their hate.

What happens when the arrogant put
others down,
As they allow gossip to trash others to
the ground?
The arrogant consider themselves wise,
Yet, truth escapes them, in disguise.

What happens when wise guidance comes
upon a land?
It enables a nation to prosper and stand.
It causes men of goodwill to rise,
Striving toward Heaven's treasured prize.

Living in the Presence of God.

Righteousness of God is acquired by faith,
Given to those who yearn to be His.
Given new life, as they freely learn to live
To His glory, honor, and praise.

Consider the price that Christ had paid.
Humbling Himself, as He hung on a cross to die;
So that those who call upon Him, Are
made alive!
His resurrection is a true sign of a living hope,
For those who are called into Him,
Will experience new and true life.
Dwelling for Eternity and forever in the
presence of God.

Walk, While There is Still Light.

As the times on earth draw near to its end,
Enclosed by darkness and with an increase of sin,
Come and walk while there is still light:
God's light.
For when the Tribulation comes, judgment
follows to put demons to flight.

Alas, for those who choose to walk in darkness,
Soon their time for redemption will end, leaving
them in their state of sin.
Yes, they will be cast away by God to never again
see the light of day.
Come and walk while there is still light, and
follow Him in His way.

Come and know the Messiah, our Lord,
Before the Tribulation reveals its sword.
Bringing upon the earth destruction and death,
Living in a state of darkness, no longer
experiencing God's breath.

Believing in Jesus.

Behold, you people, the One that you seek,
Though all-powerful, all-knowing, and ever
present, He who dwells is genuinely meek.
You do not believe, because you do not
understand,
That through His creation, everything is
controlled by His hand.

Do you not know that by believing in Jesus, you
are believing in a new and real life?
God's peace comes into you, breaking the
bondage of strife.
Be bold, by believing in Jesus, so that God may
be glorified!
Become a pleaser of God and not of man, so that
the soul may become satisfied.

In the Pursuit of Joy!

I come before You, O' Eternal God, in hopes of
singing to You, a new song.
A song that comes forth from the depths
of my heart.
Expressing the fullness of joy that is found in my
heart, of knowing that to YOU, I belong!
Holy, Holy, Holy, are You, O' God, forbid this
soul from You to depart.

As Your servant, Isaiah, had spoken years ago:
"Woe unto me, I am a man of uncleaned lips,
Living among an uncleaned people, subject to
Your judging woe…."
In the glory of Your presence, he stood amazed,
as the burning charcoal, his tongue sips.

In Your presence, Lord, what did Isaiah see?
Was it You seated upon the judgment throne?
As You continue Your creative work, what is to
come and what is to be?
As I observe Your works in my life, I declare: You,
and You alone, are GOD!
Like Isaiah, I present myself to You as being an
uncleaned man,
And as I gaze upon the empty cross and view
Your mercy seat,

I see Your Son there, advocating for me, with a
lifted hand,
seeing the forces of darkness running away in a
resounding defeat!

Lord, I come before You, with a heartfelt petition,
Requesting that You will come to give this nation
Your mercy and grace,
Because of history's continuing repetition,
We, as a people, no longer worship, by gazing
upon Your face.

Therefore, I come before You, with Your vision
in my heart,
Concerning this nation: Will You teach this
nation how to live?
As I observe this nation today, I see it has a
desire from You to depart.
My request: to see this nation be filled with the
joy of knowing You and learning how to give.

In my vision for this nation, this is what I see:
A nation turning itself toward You, with a new
founding joy;
Seeking to find real justice, graced in love,
seeking after truth, and pursuing after how life
ought to be.
Turning away from the darkness of sin, this
nation will no longer play as if it were playing
with it, like a toy.

Let this nation govern itself, like a true republic,
as it makes policy.
Rid of its national debt, to become a nation that
is financially free.
May the federal government allow states to
govern properly,
Allowing its citizens to become creative as they
learn how to be.

Replace in the hearts of men, their pursuit for
happiness, with a pursuit after joy.
So that they come to know You; they will come
with a living hope.
They will discern life's obligations like adults,
with hearts like a child,
Being regenerated in Jesus Christ because of
their newfound faith.

Faith, Free From Religion.

Lord, entwine my faith with love.
Empower me to place You above all things....
Show me the beauty that life brings.

Let my actions of faith
Be to You like a loving heart that celebrates
The bounty that You provide,
As You measure my walk in stride.

Let my religion, I pronounce, be one that shares
The love You have given to me, as to others, I give,
because I care.
May my praise to You, show of Your worthiness;
As my soul yearns for Your cleanliness.

Value of True Worship.

Install into Your people, O' Lord,
Your genuine peace.
Give to Your children, emotional release;
So that, as they come before You,
Their honor and praise to
You will be genuinely true.

Worthy are You, O' Lord, of our praise!
May the songs from our voices be raised,
To sing, hallelujah, forever and a day,
As You show us how to live each day.

Prune our hearts, as we learn to serve.
Give strength into our hands to give
You glory as You deserve.
Show Your grace and mercy through us,
as we give,
So that when others see You in us,
they will learn how to live.

Peace Comes Through Love.

Where ought we go to find peace?
A place where calm reigns and strivings cease?
Where ought we go to find anger no more?
A place where people accept each other, never
keeping score?

Soul, do you not know, that there is peace
beyond understanding,
That encompasses you with love where you
are standing?
It is found through God's Son,
Whose arms are open to everyone.
Why don't you come to find real joy?
Humble yourself before Jesus, as if you are a
girl or a boy.

Indeed, peace comes through love
Found in our Creator Father, and His Son above,
Driven by the Holy Spirit, filled with power,
Lifting us up to heights higher than any tower.

In Understanding You, O' LORD.

There is a time that comes in a man's life,
When he suddenly complains of his own
struggles and strife,
Saying: "How can this be, O' Lord,
happening to me,
This calamity of sorrow, that I see?
If only You can see things from my view—
Only then would You ask me: 'Is what you are
seeing, true?'"

Suddenly, the man comes to terms with
true reality,
Reflecting on what You have said, that's when I
discover that I am out of harmony.
I repent of my wrong way of thinking, as I turn
to focus on You.
It is then I discover that there is mystery in Your
will that shows me Your character to be true.

Causing me to say: "I now understand, O' Lord,
more clearly of Your ways,
As I now pursue with Your help to live
better my days,
O' Lord, as You lead me closer to You.
Let my compassion for You and others be sincere
and true."

A Man, Committed to God.

When a man is committed to God,
what does it look like?
Is he a man that strives to be obedient
to God's will,
Or is he a man who seeks to live in pleasure,
placing God out of sight?
How ought a man, committed to God live in
a world full of darkness?

He is the one that looks upon God
for his own salvation.
Having an Eternity placed within him,
he seeks his pleasure solely from God.
Through God's love flowing through him,
he is capable of loving others as himself,
Knowing that all of mankind is created
in His image.

He treats his helpmate with respect,
love, and grace;
And his children, enabling them to participate
with others in the human race.
He cares for the land, where God has placed him,
And works toward God being known before
his fellow man.
So they too, like him, to God will embrace
His love, with a love of their own for Him.

God's Word is My Guide.

God's Word is my guide. What more do I need?
In its pages, my soul finds spiritual food upon
which to feed.
It is like Living Water, which never runs dry,
Quenching the thirst of the soul and teaching it
how to fly.

No greater message has ever been told to man,
Which is able to cause a man, before God, to be
made right as he draws near to God and stands.
Reflecting upon the Word of God, I have
come to know
How much God's love for me is, as into
Jesus, I grow.

In My Understanding of Your Word.

Lord, as I search Your Word, I do find,
The richness of Your commandments spoken
to mankind.
Words that tell of Your love for us, which
speak of Life.
Words, that by faithfully obeying them, would
indeed put an end to human strife.

Alas, that will never be;
Because of man's sinful nature and by our works,
we can never be set free.
However, by Your grace, You have provided a way,
Through the sacrificing of Your Son, we may now
live in that Eternal glorious day.

So Lord, search my heart and cleanse the
darkness of my soul from within,
Let the mercy of Your love, rid forever my sin.
Empower me to live up to Your gift
of righteousness,
And to live for You and for others, showing them:
love, grace, and a heart of kindness.

As I worship You, Lord, may You accept the
words of my heart?

Give me the confidence to live for You, and from
Your Word, never depart.
May the joy of being Your son bring to You an
uplifting of Your glory.
And as I live, may it tell others of Your story.

Messiah, Jesus, the King.

O Messiah, Jesus, the King,
You are the God of Eternal life.
Into Your House, the saints You will bring.
And when we are there, we, to You, will sing:

"Lamb of God, You are the Lord and King,
Father God has given You everything.
Worthy are You to forever be praised!
As it is for this purpose our voices be raised!"

We are the light shining in the darkness,
Seeking to find a place to put Your lamp,
So the dead may come to life, seeking Your
kindness, as they turn from their dark ways into
Your righteousness.
With a new-given life, we are now set free
To live for You as we ought, as into You, we
learn to be.

Lamb of God, You are the Lord and King,
Father God has given You everything.
Worthy are You to forever be praised!
As it is for this purpose, our voices be raised.

We are the salt of the world, giving it flavor,
So the dead of the world will discover new life.
As they respond to Your loving call and favor.

Empowered by the Holy Spirit with joy, their
new life they will savor.
We sing, "Glory to God for the forgiveness of sin,
As we repent of our old ways, so that into Your
Kingdom, we may enter in."

Lamb of God, You are the Lord and King,
Father God has given You everything.
Worthy are You to forever be praised!
As it is for this purpose, our voices be raised.

We are the living hope to those who are
spiritually blind,
Placed here by the solid ROCK, who is our
Living Christ.
We seek Christ, those who are lost, so that by the
Spirit of God, they may be found.
Bringing them into the fold of God, set upon
Holy Ground.
Upon a cross, Jesus paid the price,
So that dead men can find forgiveness and
have new life.

Lamb of God, You are the Lord and King.
Father God has given You everything.
Worthy are You to forever be praised!
As it is for this purpose, our voices be raised.

We are the children of God, being made right,

Justified by God the Father, because of the
sacrifice made.
Behold, the Lamb of God, is now in sight.
He won the battle over sin and death, as He has
given us new life.
And to those who yearn to be His, and learn
of His ways,
Eternity will come to them, forever and a day.

Lamb of God, You are the Lord and King.
Father God has given You everything.
Worthy are You to forever be praised!
As it is for this purpose, our voices be raised.

Testifying to GOD'S Awesome BEING.

I give testimony, O' Lord, who is Creator
of all things.
I come before You, declaring You to be Lord, yes,
You are my King.
There is nothing greater than You, Lord, the
giver of life.
To all who come to You, at Your calling,
You put an end to their strife.
Empower us all to worship You, all of our days;
And give us power and guidance to always walk
in Your ways.

Essence of Our Being.

Lord, as I ponder upon the essence of our being,
What is it that You desire for us to be seeing?
Living in the midst of darkness, longing for
Your light,
How long must we wait before receiving Your
perfect sight?

In Your image, it is clear to us that You
have a plan.
A purpose, which You have fixed, as we travel
towards Eternity Land;
A comfort to us, as You prepare our souls to
listen and be taught.
Your Son has provided a way, we have been
purchased—yes—we have been bought.

In Your Kingdom, Your Son has prepared a place,
Making way to be able to see You face-to-face.
Having a design for us beyond human
understanding,
For those who have received You, Eternally
serving You, is in all of Your planning.

SECTION FOUR:

DISCOVERING GOD'S WISDOM

CONCLUDING DEVOTION:

True Meaning of Religion.

"I waited patiently for the Lord;
He inclined to me and heard my cry.
He drew me up from the pit of destruction,
out of the miry bog,
and set my feet upon a rock,
making my steps secure.
He puts a new song in my mouth,
a song of praise to our God.
Many will see and fear, and put
their trust in the Lord.

Blessed is the man who makes the Lord his trust
Who does not turn to the proud, to those who
go astray after a lie!

You have multiplied, O' Lord, my God, your
wondrous deeds and Your thoughts toward us,
None can compare with YOU! I will proclaim
them, yet they are more than can be told.
(Ps 40: 1-5 ESV).

What then, is the true meaning of religion? Is
it about a ritual dance before the Lord, in hopes
of finding His favor? Is it about doing more good
works than doing evil? Is it about making sacrifices
in order to have our sins covered?

No, it is none of this. True religion is found in
the person who fears the Lord, who seeks justice
for his neighbor, and offers grace and mercy to
those who are lost, seeking to be found. It is in the
passion of the believer in Christ, Jesus, to share the
faith with others, in hopes that they will obtain
the level of faith as is found in the one, sharing
the faith.

The prophet Micah made this observation, in
what God requires of us as we walk with Him:
"Israel speaking: 'What should I bring into the
presence of the Eternal One to pay homage to
the God Most High? Should I come into His
presence with burnt offerings, with year-old
calves to sacrifice? Would the Eternal be pleased
by thousands of sacrificial rams, by ten thousand
swollen rivers of olive oil? Should I offer my oldest

son for my wrongdoing, the child of my body to cover the sins of my life?'

'No, He has told you, mortals, what is good in His sight: What else does the Eternal ask of you but to live justly and to love kindness and to walk with your True GOD in all humility?'

'The voice of the Eternal cries out to the city of Jerusalem and the wise fear Your name.'"(Mi.6:6-9 The Voice.)

PRAYER: Heavenly Father, may the reader be blessed by the poetic and the devotional messages written in this book. May the reader come to know You more, Lord Jesus, and receive You into the reader's heart. May the reader grow in faith and acquire an intimacy with You, far greater than that found in me. May the power of the Holy Spirit strengthen the walk of the reader, and boldly proclaim You to others. Let the wisdom of the poems here speak to their hearts, so that the reader may walk wisely in You, trusting only in Your wisdom. In Jesus's Name. YES!

Seeking After Wisdom.

O' man, do you hear the Voice of Lady Wisdom,
Yearning for you to seek after Her way?
She yearns for justice, pointing Her followers
to God's kingdom.
Adorning them with riches, which last for all
of their days!

She bestows Her love to all who loves Her
And Her rewards last throughout Eternity.
She offers peace through rightful living
that endures,
Prodding Christ's followers toward a
common community.
To the wise, earthly treasures are given—
A prelude to what is to come when meeting the
Most High.
Through a sincere following after Christ, sins
are forgiven.
"Finally, a time will come, when the wise will
meet God in the sky."

Be Wise.

Be wise to the ways of the Lord.
For into your hand, He will give you a sword,
To fight against the wicked living in darkness.
He will give life, to show others kindness.

Let not the pride for living
Interfere with your ability for giving
Of yourselves to others in love,
Instead, with your life, point to Jesus Who reigns
from above.

Be humble before your Master and King.
Anticipate with joy at what He will bring:
Salvation to those who call upon Jesus's name—
Live, by the power of His grace,
And your life will never be the same.
Run toward God, and experience His embrace.

In Finding True Happiness.

In living in the way of being wise,
Brings one to a place called happiness.
He is the one who seeks after the prize
And discovers from his journey that he is no
longer restless.

By discerning the truth from folly, he
discovers joy.
Although he lives in a broken world, full of pain,
He's the one who fears God and lives life,
like a boy.
With love in his heart, he rejoices in God's reign.

As he listens to the teachings of Lady Wisdom,
and adheres to her ways,
He acknowledges the importance of all his
relationships.
He also seeks God's purposes for him, as he lives
out his days,
Seeking to find time with God and man in which
to fellowship.

In Awe of You!

Fear of the Lord, by God's chosen people,
Is indeed their strength.
For by God's creative hand,
He caused man, before Him, to stand.
In reverence, the redeemed, are able to see
God's glory and greatness.
It is because of His mighty and creative hand.
He allows all of mankind to be.

In awe of You, O' Lord,
We can't help but wonder,
As to the "why's" of Your creation
That enable us to be.
In our faith in You,
We are made right through the sacrifice
of Your Son.
Indeed, He is Your Anointed One,
Who, by Your loving grace,
Has given us Eternal life,
As we live in Your embrace.

Last Prayer.

Heavenly Father, I dedicate this book to YOU.

May it bring a blessing to those who read these pages.

In Jesus's Name. Amen.

Work Cited Page

All poems are a reflection from Scriptures without any direct quotes.

The two main versions used in the book are: the ESV and The Voice/Compass Bible.

Scripture verses used:

Section One:
Jn.14:1-6 ESV
Jn.3:16 ESV

Section Two:
Rev. 22:14-17 ESV

Section Three:
Mt. 5:14-16

Section Four:
Ps. 40:1-5 ESV
Mi. 6: 6-9 The Voice/Compass Bible.

CPSIA information can be obtained
at www.ICGtesting.com
Printed in the USA
BVHW070754221221
624594BV00009B/656

9 781662 835889